英汉对照管理袖珍手册

管理变革

Neil Russell-Jones 著
刘　恋　　　　译
Phil Hailstone 图

上海交通大学出版社

图书在版编目(CIP)数据

管理变革/(英)琼斯(Jones, N. R)著;刘恋译 . 一上海:上海交通大学出版社,2002(2011 重印)

(英汉对照管理袖珍手册)

ISBN 978-7-313-02933-1

Ⅰ.管… Ⅱ.① 琼… ② 刘… Ⅲ.管理学-对照读物-英、汉 Ⅳ.C93

中国版本图书馆 CIP 数据核字(2001)第 094777 号

责任编辑 杨 鹏

英汉对照管理袖珍手册:管理变革

Neil Russell-Jones 著

上海交通大学出版社出版发行

(上海市番禺路 951 号 邮政编码 200030)

电话:64071208 出版人:韩建民

常熟市梅李印刷有限公司印刷 全国新华书店经销

开本:890mm×1240mm 1/64 印张:3.375 字数:102 千字

2002 年 2 月第 1 版 2011 年 4 月第 4 次印刷

印数:13 151~15 180

ISBN 978-7-313-02933-1/C · 06 定价:10.00 元

CONTENTS

目　录

恐龙灭绝了!哺乳动物没有!

相反它们接受了变革并存活至今。

INTRODUCTION
导　言

INTRODUCTION

Change is with us and will always be here, and there are two ways of dealing with it:

- **Reactively,** by responding only when one has to, usually too late

- **Proactively,** by planning for change and trying to keep, if not one step ahead, then at least in the vanguard of change

Of course, there is a third option - ignore it and hope it will go away. This was the course followed by dinosaurs, dodos and many companies that could not read the writing on the wall (eg: British motor bike manufacturers which were devoured by the Japanese onslaught).

变革将永远存在,并且与我们形影相随。对待变革的方式有两种:

● **应激反应**,只在迫不得已时才作出反应,往往已经为时过晚

● **超前反应**,为打造变革提前计划准备并且持之以恒,即使不能够领先一步,至少也要成为变革的先驱

当然还有第三种选择——完全无视变革,希望它会自行消失。这也正是已经灭绝了的恐龙、渡渡鸟(产于毛里求斯的一种巨鸟,已绝种,译注)和许多对颠覆的征兆熟视无睹的公司所选择的道路(例如:在日本同类产品的猛烈进攻之下遭受毁灭性打击的英国摩托车制造业)。

INTRODUCTION

Change and change programmes are, however, necessarily difficult and complex to manage, and even, sometimes, to understand.

The objective of this book is to clarify the key elements in the process, including the problems, pitfalls, solutions and the assistance available to those involved in change programmes. You may be an active participant, or on the receiving end, or you may just wish to understand more about it.

This book will not make you into a change expert but it will, we hope, give a good understanding of the basics and serve as an introduction to the process of change.

　　然而,成功地实施变革以及变革的方案必定艰难而复杂,有时甚至理解它们都很困难、很复杂。

　　本书着力于阐明整个变革过程中的诸多关键因素,包含问题、陷阱、解决方案以及具体实施步骤中可能获得的帮助。你可以是一个管理变革的积极参与者,也可以只是一味地接受变革,或者你仅仅希望对变革了解得更多一些。

　　本书并不能够将你塑造成为一个变革专家,但是我们希望它能够把管理变革的基本原理阐释得清楚明白,并且成为一本关于变革过程的入门初阶。

NOTES
笔 记

⑥

WHAT IS CHANGE?
变革是什么?

WHAT IS CHANGE?

DEFINITIONS

Noun - Making or becoming different
- Difference from previous state
- Substitution of one for another
- Variation

Verb - To undergo, show or subject to change
- To make or become different

The emphasis is on making something different. This could be a major change or merely incremental. Whichever it is implies a difference:

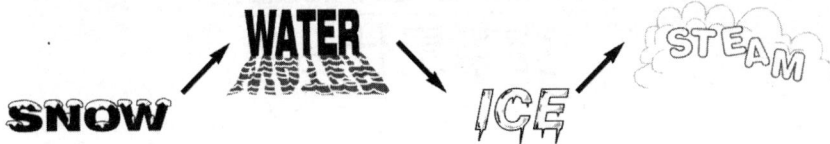

变革是什么？

定义

名词——制造或呈现出的差异
　　　——与先前不同的状态
　　　——一对一的替换
　　　——变化

动词——承受、展现成顺应变化
　　　——制造或呈现差异

　　重点在于使事物变得不同。下图可以说是一个突破式的变革或者仅仅是一些分步完成的变化，但不管怎么说它都意味着差异：

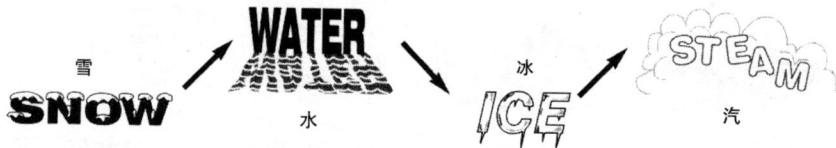

WHAT IS CHANGE?

ANNUAL CHANGE CYCLE

There is major change all around you.

Each year the earth goes through an enormous change caused by its rotation (more perceptible in some parts than others) which forces responses that are staggering in enormity. For example, deciduous trees shed their leaves and close down for winter, to bloom again in spring; and animals change their coats (mink/ermine).

Think, too, of the way in which we humans have to respond to climatic changes, by varying our clothing at different times of the year or by regulating the heating or air conditioning. Our well-being depends upon managing such changes.

SPRING   SUMMER   FALL/AUTUMN   WINTER

变革是什么？
年度变化循环

在你周围就有着突破式的变化。

每年地球都要经历一次由它的自转(在某些地方比其他地方更明显)而带来的巨大变革，回应这种周期循环的大量变化应运而生。例如：落叶乔木为了度过冬天散落它们的叶子，但第二年春天又会重新萌芽开花；动物们也变换着它们的"外套"(比如貂与貂皮)。

再联想一下我们人类对于气候变化的反应，在一年中不同的时间里我们变换着不同的服饰，有时打开暖气，有时又摆弄空调。我们的幸福安康正取决于我们对这些变化的成功把握。

春　　　　　夏　　　　　秋　　　　　冬

WHAT IS CHANGE?

INCREMENTAL CHANGE

The change from manual recording of information (writing) to current laptops with advanced capability is an enormous one. In fact, it occurred incrementally through several steps.

| **Ancient** | **19th C** | **early 1900s** | **mid 1900s** | **1980s** | **1990s** |

Each step is incremental, requiring skills training and capital outlay.

The change in information processing was even greater, from scrolls to libraries to main frames to midis to LANs.

变革是什么?
渐进式变革

从信息的手写记录 (执笔书写) 到今天高性能的笔记本电脑, 这之间的变革无异于翻天覆地。但事实上, 这种巨大的变革是分若干步逐级提升的。

| 古代 | 19 世纪 | 20 世纪早期 | 20 世纪中期 | 20 世纪 80 年代 | 20 世纪 90 年代 |

每一步都是渐进式的, 都需要技术的培训和资本的消耗。

从最初的卷轴书到图书馆到主机机枢、音乐设备数字界面, 直到今天的计算机局域网络, 信息处理方式的变革更是日新月异。

WHAT IS CHANGE?

METAMORPHOSIS

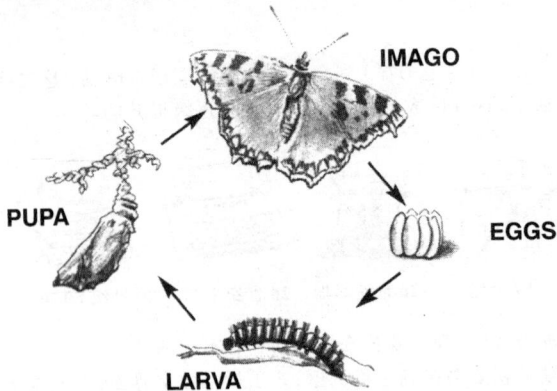

IMAGO

PUPA

EGGS

LARVA

Change can be of an even greater nature. Consider metamorphosis, for example, which requires a complete change of state and represents a severe shock to the status quo (in this case requiring a sleeping phase to cope with the change).

(14)

变革是什么?
变态发育

    变革可以更为剧烈。以变态发育为例,它需要一种对现存状态的根本性变革,象征着对于现状的一次重大冲击(在这种情况下一段休眠期对于应付变革是十分必要的)。

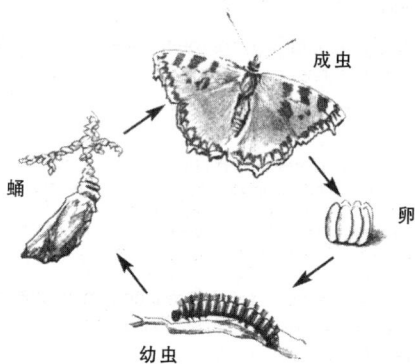

成虫

蛹

卵

幼虫

WHAT IS CHANGE?

ORGANISATIONAL

Incremental change:

- <u>10% decrease in staff</u> (usually achieved by natural wastage and early retirement; therefore non-threatening)

- <u>Introduction of performance-related pay</u> (can be threatening for those who might underperform or perceive that they might)

Major change:

- <u>25%+ reduction in staff</u> (commonly involving large-scale redundancies/closures/ relocation and leading to great fear and uncertainty and therefore great resistance)

- <u>Premises rationalisation</u> (usually results in changed work environments in terms of place and benefits)

- <u>Disinvestment/acquisition</u> (usually leads to great fear and uncertainty which can cause it to fail; GEC's bid for Siemens was halted by the staff in Germany fearing for their jobs because of the likelihood of rationalisation)

变革是什么?
企业变革

渐进式变革

- <u>员工削减 10%</u>（通常可以通过自然资源闲置和提早退休来达到，因而不具有威胁性）
- <u>导入与业绩挂钩的薪酬机制</u>（可以对那些业绩不佳或意识到自身业绩可能不佳的员工形成压力）

突破式变革

- <u>员工削减 25% 以上</u>（通常包含着大规模的减少冗员、关闭分支机构或是重组部门，一般会带来巨大的恐慌和不稳定感，因此会遭到强烈的抵制）
- <u>办事机构合理化</u>（通常会导致工作环境的改变，这里所说的工作环境指的是工作地点和收益）
- <u>收回投资/收购</u>（通常会引起巨大的恐慌和心理震荡，而这些因素可能导致失败；通用电器公司放弃收购西门子公司就是因为通用在德员工担心两家公司合并后可能引发的合理化重组会给他们的现有职位带来影响）

CHANGE IN BUSINESS

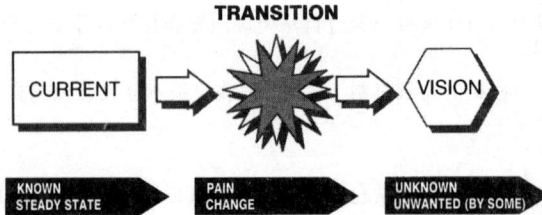

TRANSITION

| CURRENT | ⇨ | TRANSITION | ⇨ | VISION |

| KNOWN STEADY STATE | PAIN CHANGE | UNKNOWN UNWANTED (BY SOME) |

Change management is the process of moving from the current state to the `vision' of the future and involves a degree of transition which may also result in `pain' for some or, more commonly, all.

商业变革

转变

现状 → 远景

众所周知的
稳定状态

痛苦
变革

无法预知的
不受欢迎的(对某些人而言)

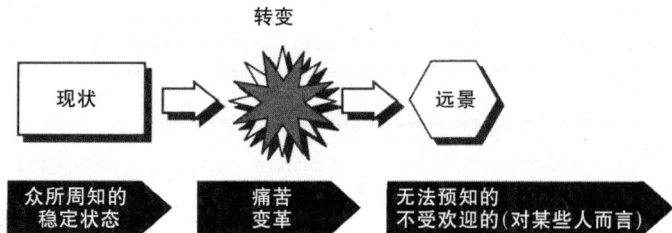

管理的变革就是从现行状态到达"远景目标"的变革过程,其中所蕴涵的一定程度的转变对某些人而言可能是"痛苦的",有时这种痛苦会更普遍一些,波及到全体员工。

WHAT DRIVES CHANGE?

What <u>doesn't</u> drive change is the attitude that, `**If it ain't broke, don't fix it**'.
Yes, `it' may be working now but is it doing so sufficiently well and will it do so in the future?
You may need to reconsider the meaning of the term `ain't broke'.

Change has many causes, for example:

- Ice Age forced adaptation (hairy mammoth, man discovered how to use caves, skins and fire)

In business change is influenced by, for example:

- New competition
- Price changes
- Technology
- Regulation
- Consumer demand

**ADAPT
OR DIE
COPY, MATCH
OR INNOVATE**

变革是什么?
什么导致变革?

那种**"不破,不修"**的态度是不会导致变革的。

的确,现行状态可能在目前是有效的,但它达到足够高效了吗?它在未来也会保持同等程度吗?

你可能需要重新思考一下**"不破"**这个短语的涵义了。

造成变革的原因有许多,比如:

- 冰河时代的被动适应(多毛的猛犸象,人类发现如何利用洞穴、兽皮和火)

商业领域的变革也受到一些因素的影响,比如:

- 新的竞争
- 价格的改变
- 技术
- 经济调控
- 消费需求

变革
或者死亡
模仿,适应
抑或创新

CHANGE DRIVERS

There are many drivers, both internal and external, that force changes on an organisation.

变革是什么?
变革动力

一个企业的变革会由许多因素造成,包括内部动因和外部动因。

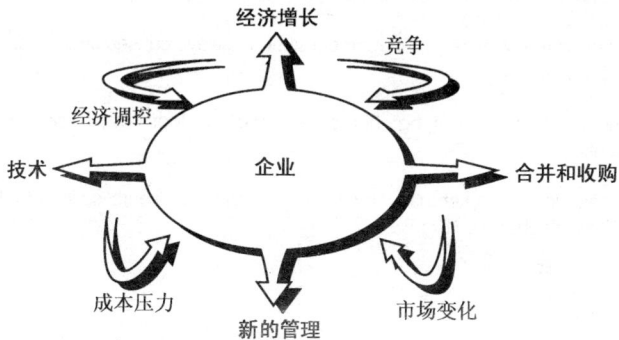

经济增长

竞争

经济调控

技术

企业

合并和收购

成本压力

新的管理

市场变化

WHAT IS CHANGE?

CHANGE DRIVERS

Factors driving change include:

- New shareholders may force a change as with the Chase Manhattan Bank in 1995

- The appointment of new management almost always causes change as the `new broom sweeps clean'

- Competition may force it, eg: home delivery of fast food (pizza), direct insurance sales or banking

- A change in the market may force it, eg: privatisation, liberalisation of rules (telecoms, UK Stock Exchange, `Big Bang')

变革是什么?
变革动力

变革的动因包括:

- 新的股东可能会带来一场变革,Chase Manhattan 银行 1995 年即是如此
- 新的管理层的任命几乎总是带来变动,就好像"新官上任三把火"
- 竞争可能会带来变革,例如:快餐的送货上门(披萨饼),直接的保险销售或者银行业务
- 市场上的变革可能会导致变革,例如:私有化,自由化(电信业,英国证券交易行业,"大震")

WHAT IS CHANGE?

BURNING PLATFORM

Typically there must be a `burning platform' to cause the change to accepted practices.

This phrase comes from the Piper Alpha disaster in the North Sea where the only survivors were those who leapt off the rig **in defiance of instructions** and into the sea which was freezing cold and alight with oil. The burning platform forced a reappraisal of existing rules and the status quo.

For a company, the burning platform could be a combination of things or one overriding concern, eg: disclosure of commissions in Life and Pensions transactions.

变革是什么?
燃烧平台

　　通常情况下一定会有一个"燃烧平台"给现行惯例带来变革。

　　这个短语来源于北海油田的 Piper Alpha 灾难，在那次灾难中仅有的幸存者是那些**无视命令**跳离钻井架、纵身跃入海中的人，虽然当时的海水冰冷刺骨、表面的油层熊熊燃烧。燃烧平台促使我们不得不对现行规则和当前状况作出一个重新的评估。

　　对一家公司而言，燃烧的平台可以是一大堆事情或是出于一个重要性高于一切的考虑，例如：人寿保险和养老金保险交易中佣金的披露。

WHY CHANGE?

For your organisation, list the reasons why it might have to change:

_____

_____

_____

_____

_____

_____

_____

_____

变革是什么?
为何变革?

针对你的公司,列举出它必须变革的原因:

_____

_____

_____

_____

_____

_____

_____

WHAT IS CHANGE?

HOW TO CHANGE

Having listed the reasons **why** your organisation might have to change, now list **how** it might change:

_____

_____

_____

_____

_____

_____

_____

_____

变革是什么?
怎样变革

列出你的公司**为什么**必须变革的原因之后,现在再来列出它可能**怎样**变革:

_____

_____

_____

_____

_____

_____

_____

_____

WHAT IS CHANGE?

WHY CHANGE?

EXAMPLES

Life company

- Increasing competition from banks, direct sales operations
- Disclosure of policy costs to public
- Change by customers to other, unregulated, products

Retailer

- Change in consumer preferences (eg: vegetarianism)
- Climatic changes (warmer winters lead to less demand for, eg: furs)
- Out of town outlets put pressure on smaller independent retailers
- Opening up of the single European market increases competition

变革是什么?
为何变革?
实例

人寿保险公司
- 越来越多来自银行的、直接保险销售竞争
- 保单费用被披露
- 顾客转向购买其他没有政府管制的商品

零售商
- 顾客喜好的转变(例如:素食主义)
- 气候的变化(暖冬使得人们对某些商品的需求减少,比如:毛皮)
- 本商业区外的经销商对较小的独立零售商的压力
- 单一欧洲市场的开放加剧了市场竞争

WHAT IS CHANGE?

WHY CHANGE?
EXAMPLES

Manufacturer

- Competition has reduced costs by say 35%
- Cheaper overseas producers
- Technological developments render products obsolete
- New environmental/safety rules

Public sector

- Impending privatisation
- Government imposing market forces onto it

变革是什么?

为何变革?

实例

制造商

- 竞争使成本降低了据说 35%
- 便宜的海外商品
- 技术进步导致产品被淘汰
- 新的环境/安全法规

公用领域

- 私有化初露端倪
- 政府强行把市场力量纳入其中

HOW TO CHANGE

EXAMPLES

Life company

- Reduce expenses portion of costs
- Reappraise distribution channels
- Offer new products, form joint ventures

Retailer

- Offer new products, advertise in new markets
- Change stock to reflect environment, change perception of goods to fashion rather than necessities
- Form town loyalty cards, link with others to increase price leverage in purchasing
- Export goods, negotiate with importers so as to offer same goods as competitors

变革是什么?
怎样变革
实例

人寿保险公司
- 降低成本中经费所占的份额
- 重新评估销售渠道
- 提供新产品,共同承担风险

零售商
- 提供新商品,为新市场做宣传
- 根据市场环境调整商品库存,根据流行时尚而非生活必需改变商品理念
- 建立城区忠诚卡,与其他零售商结成同盟,增进商品买卖中价格杠杆的作用
- 向国外输出商品,与进口商谈判以便能够提供与竞争对手相似的产品

HOW TO CHANGE
EXAMPLES

Manufacturer

- Review overheads and cut
- Source overseas/invest in technology
- Change products/invest in technology/produce next generation products

Public sector

- Prepare staff by introducing norms and management performance
- Consult staff and explain changes
- Recruit external staff from private sector

No matter which actions are chosen, there are potentially enormous implications. Therefore, there is a need to manage the change in an effective manner.

怎样变革

实例

制造商

- 审核管理费用和削减日常开支
- 海外资源/技术投资
- 产品变革/技术投资/开发换代产品

公用领域

- 引入规范和业绩管理从而使自己的员工做好准备
- 与员工协商并向其解释变革
- 从私营领域招募外部员工

不管采取哪种方式,都可能会产生深远的意义。因而,以一种行之有效的方式驾驭变革是十分必要的。

NOTES
笔 记

PREPARING FOR CHANGE
变革总动员

MAKING IT HAPPEN

Making change happen involves:

- Moving an organisation's
    - people, and
    - culture

- In line with an organisation's
    - structure   -   strategy
    - processes   -   systems

Such that change is successful and delivers long-lasting benefit to the organisation!

This is not easy and, therefore, requires a process to assist in the management. This is what **Change Management** is all about.

変革总动员
造就变革

造就变革包括：

● 变动一家企业的

——人员,以及

——文化

● 立足于一家企业的

——结构　　　　　　——战略

——流程　　　　　　——系统

这样的变革才会成功并且给企业带来长久的利益!

　　但这并非轻而易举,因而在实际管理中需要一个过程去促成变革。而这正是**变革管理**所要做的。

SUCCESSFUL CHANGE MANAGEMENT

COMMITMENT

Successful Change Management is about **taking the people with you**.

DOCK

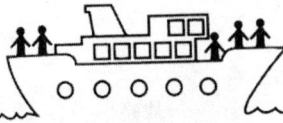

HMS ORGANISATION

VISION / OPPORTUNITY

Unless the people in an organisation - at all levels, from senior management to employees - are committed to the change, then it will fail. This is not an option and without this commitment any project is doomed.

変革总动员

成功的变革管理

赞同与拥护

    <u>成功的管理变革是要**使所有人与你同舟共济**。</u>

    除非一个企业中的员工——包括各个层次，从高级管理层到普通员工——都对变革达成一致，否则变革便会半途夭折。这种普遍认同是没有选择余地的，失去它任何计划都难逃失败的命运。

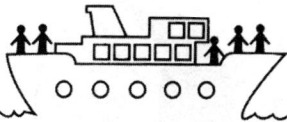

| 船坞 | 英国皇家海军舰艇式的企业 | 远景/机遇 |

PREPARING FOR CHANGE

SUCCESSFUL CHANGE MANAGEMENT
POSITIONING

You must position the change project in the right place to maximise successful implementation.

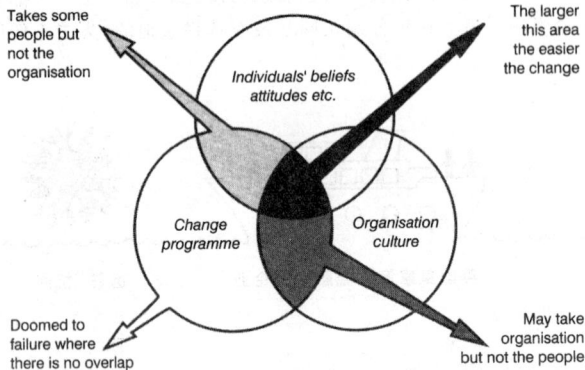

Takes some people but not the organisation

Individuals' beliefs attitudes etc.

The larger this area the easier the change

Change programme

Organisation culture

Note: It will be different for different individuals and different parts of the organisation.

Doomed to failure where there is no overlap

May take organisation but not the people

成功的变革管理

定位

你必须把变革的方案安置在合适的位置以使它发挥最大的效力。

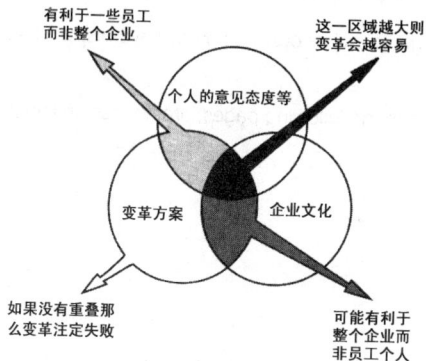

有利于一些员工
而非整个企业

这一区域越大则
变革会越容易

个人的意见态度等

变革方案　　企业文化

如果没有重叠那
么变革注定失败

可能有利于
整个企业而
非员工个人

注意：针对企业里不同的个人与不同的部门变革方案将会有所不同。

SUCCESSFUL CHANGE MANAGEMENT
EXPERT VIEWS

Much research has already been carried out into change.

Several management gurus are recognised; many have distilled their findings down to a number of key points.

Their findings, outlined on the following pages, are not cast in tablets of stone but do serve as useful reminders.

变革总动员

成功的管理变革
专家观点

　　大量针对变革的深入研究已经展开。

　　许多管理权威是大家公认的;他们中的一些还把自己的发现精炼为一些关键点。

　　他们的发现(后面的几页中有其大致摘要)虽然不是金科玉律但肯定会带来一些有益的启示。

CONDITIONS FOR SUCCESS

EXPERT VIEWS

Rosabeth Moss Kantor is a professor at Harvard who has carried out research into change. These are her 10 Commandments:

1   Analyse the organisation and its need for change
2   Create a shared vision and common direction
3   Separate from the past
4   Create a sense of urgency
5   Support a strong leadership role
6   Line up political sponsorship
7   Craft an implementation plan
8   Develop enabling structures
9   Communicate and involve people
10 Reinforce and institutionalise change

What she is saying is:

- Look at what you have got
- Obtain buy-in at all levels
- Plan the change, and
- Put in place a structure for implementing it
- Finally, make people live and breathe change

成功必备

专家观点

罗莎贝斯·莫斯·坎特是哈佛大学的一名教授,她曾对变革作过深入研究。这些是她的十条戒律:

1. 分析企业及其变革的需要
2. 创立一个普遍认同的远景和共同的方向
3. 与以往决裂
4. 形成一种紧迫感

5. 扶持一位强有力的领导者
6. 列出政府资助项目
7. 设计一个执行方案
8. 发展可行的组织结构
9. 与员工沟通并把他们引入变革
10. 加强变革并使之制度化

她的格言是:

- 查看你已经拥有的
- 获得各个方面的普遍认同
- 拟订变革方案,并且

- 合理定位执行变革的结构
- 最后,使员工长久沐浴在变革之中

CONDITIONS FOR SUCCESS

EXPERT VIEWS

Organisational Development Resources Inc, an American organisation established by Daryl Connor and specialising in change management, has built up an extensive database on change. Its four determinants are:

1 Sponsor commitment   3 Target resistance
2 Agent skills   4 Cultural alignment

The point here is:

- To make sure that there is someone championing the change who has the authority to make it happen

- To put people in place to make it happen

- To concentrate on those who resist most (the other side of the bell curve - see page 90), and

- To try to make the changes in accordance with usual practice, to make people feel as comfortable as possible

成功必备
专家观点

企业发展资源公司，是由达里尔·科勒创建的一家专门从事变革管理研究的美国机构，在变革领域它已经逐步建立起一个涵盖很广的数据库。它的四大决定因素如下：

1　发起者的承诺　　　　　　3　变革阻力
2　代理人的技巧　　　　　　4　文化联盟

这里的要点是：

- 确保变革的领导者拥有促成变革的权力
- 合理安排员工以促成变革
- 集中注意那些激烈抵制变革的人(钟形曲线的另一面——参考第 90 页)，以及
- 尝试使变革与通常的做事方式相协调，使员工尽可能感觉舒适

CONDITIONS FOR SUCCESS
EXPERT VIEWS

Beckhard, erstwhile professor at M.I.T. (USA), notes seven conditions for success:

1 Organisational vision and direction towards the vision
2 A clear sense of the organisation's identity
3 Understanding of the organisation's external relationships
4 Clear and reachable scenarios
5 Flexible structures
6 Effective use of technology
7 Rewards that harmonise people with the organisation's objectives

The key points here are:

● Understand your organisation and its relationships
● Be flexible
● Have a vision, and
● A map to get there

成功必备
专家观点

贝克哈德,前麻省理工学院(美国)教授,提出成功的七条原则:

1　企业的远景目标以及通往
　　目标的管理
2　对企业本身的清晰把握
3　了解企业的外部关联

4　清楚可行的方案
5　灵活的结构
6　技术的有效运用
7　通过奖励机制来使
　　员工与企业的目标相一致

这里的要点是:

- 了解你的企业和它的联系
- 保持灵活

- 拥有一个远景目标,以及
- 达到目标的具体方案

CONDITIONS FOR SUCCESS
SUMMARY OF EXPERT VIEWS

Each of the gurus has examined change and broadly come to the same conclusions:

- It is very difficult
- The further you go the harder it becomes
- The less that the change has in common with the organisation's culture, the less likely success is
- It needs a strong, important sponsor
- A body of people dedicated to making it happen is essential
- Communication is the key

成功必备

专家观点的简要概括

每一位专家都考察了变革并大致形成了以下相似的结论：

- 变革相当困难
- 变革难度与变革的深入程度成正比
- 变革与企业文化的重叠越少则成功的可能性也就越小
- 它需要一个强有力的、显要的支持者
- 一支致力于促成变革的团队是必不可少的
- 沟通是关键

CONDITIONS FOR SUCCESS
AIDE MEMOIRE

Make sure that your change programme is a **SUCCESS** by following these principles:

Shared vision

Understand the organisation

Cultural alignment

Communication

Experienced help where necessary

Strong leadership

Stakeholder buy-in

变革总动员

成功必备

辅助备忘录

遵循这些原则以确保你的变革方案获得**成功**：
普遍认同的远景
了解企业
文化整合
沟通
必要时经验丰富的帮手
强有力的领导
赌金持有者的买进

CONDITIONS FOR SUCCESS
THE 'SUCCESS' PRINCIPLE

YES!

S
U
C
C
E
S
S

Shared vision

Ensure that there is a clear statement as to where the change is taking you and that it is understood by everyone

60

成功必备
"SUCCESS"原则

成

功

普遍认同的远景

确保就变革的诱人之处作一个清晰的阐述并使之深入人心

变革总动员
成功必备
"SUCCESS"原则

成

功

> 了解企业
>
> 分析企业以找出它的主要特征和需要特别关注的地方

CONDITIONS FOR SUCCESS

THE 'SUCCESS' PRINCIPLE

YES!

S
U
C
C
E
S
S

Cultural alignment

Try to ensure that change is made in ways that are close to the way things are normally done

(64)

变革总动员

成功必备

"SUCCESS"原则

成

功

文化整合

尝试使变革能够贴近于人们通常做事的方式

CONDITIONS FOR SUCCESS
THE 'SUCCESS' PRINCIPLE

S
U
C
C
E
S
S

Communication

Communicate as soon as possible and where there is something to say (see `Communication' chapter)

66

成功必备

"SUCCESS"原则

成

> 沟通
>
> 尽可能及时地沟通，在需要说明的地方进行交流（参看"沟通"一章）

功

CONDITIONS FOR SUCCESS
THE 'SUCCESS' PRINCIPLE

YES!

S
U
C
C
E
S
S

Experienced help where necessary

Use appropriate methodologies that have been tried and tested, to ensure that your programme will deliver what you want and not surprises; if this means using external help, then do not be afraid to do so

68

成功必备

"SUCCESS"原则

成

功

必要时经验丰富的帮手

借鉴已被尝试并验证为合适的方法论,以确保你的方案能够传达出你的愿望并且使它不会惊世骇俗;如果这将意味着借助外部的帮助,不要因为担心而裹足不前

成功必备

"SUCCESS"原则

成

功

强有力的领导

一个强有力的公司最高层人物应该支持变革并且把这种支持显示出来；他应该为一个目标——方案的成功——作出贡献

CONDITIONS FOR SUCCESS

THE 'SUCCESS' PRINCIPLE

YES!

S
U
C
C
E
S
S
S

Stakeholder buy-in

Ensure that anyone with a `stake' in the programme has bought-in. Stakeholders can be:

- employees   - management
- shareholders - suppliers
- government

(72)

成功必备
"SUCCESS"原则

成

功

赌金持有者的买进

确保任何一个在变革方案中拥有"赌注"
的人都会买进。赌金持有者可以是：
- ——雇员　　——管理层
- ——股东　　——供应商
- ——政府

PREPARING FOR CHANGE

BARRIERS

A change programme will affect the way an organisation works. Two factors must be considered **before** implementation:

- Culture
  - how an organisation operates; the change programme will almost certainly be counter cultural in some way

- People
  - how people will receive the change and the actions they might take to resist it

The two are inextricably linked.

変革总动员
变革的障碍

YES!

　　一个变革方案将会影响到一个企业的运作方式。在实施变革前有两个因素必须被考虑到:

- 文化
  - —— 一家企业如何运作;变革方案几乎一定会以某种方式遭遇到企业文化
- 员工
  - —— 员工将如何接受变革以及他们可能采取的抵制行动

这两点与变革不可避免地联系在一起。

BARRIERS

A recent survey in the US* found that the biggest obstacles to change were, in descending order of priority:

- Employee resistance
- Inappropriate culture
- Poor communication/plan
- Incomplete follow-up
- Lack of management agreement on strategy
- Insufficient skills

William Schiemann and Associates Inc.

变革的障碍

在美国,一次最近的调查研究发现变革中最大的阻力可以按照降序排列为:

- 雇员的抵制
- 不适宜的文化
- 糟糕的沟通／计划
- 不完备的后续工作
- 在战略部署方面缺乏管理层的认同
- 不充足的技能

* 威廉·斯希曼合众公司。

BARRIERS

Where barriers exist, they must be negated, got round or climbed over. This means understanding the culture, readiness to change and the people.

YES!

变革的障碍

YES!

　　哪里存在阻力，就应该在哪里消灭它、绕过它或者跨越它。这意味着对文化、变革的准备以及员工的把握。

WHAT IS CULTURE?

- The way that things are done in an organisation (or nation)
- What is acceptable and what is not
- Overt and covert rules/mores/norms that guide behaviour

Compare:

- clearing bank
- investment bank

- civil service
- retail organisation

- nationalised company
- privatised company (in same sectors)

文化是什么?

- 在一个企业(国家)里做事的方式
- 什么是可以接受的而什么不是
- 外在的和潜在的引导行为的准则/习俗/规范

对比:

—结算银行

—投资银行

—公众服务

—零售企业

—国有企业

—私有企业(在相同行业)

WHY LOOK AT CULTURE?

It is important to understand the culture of an organisation in order to understand how best to implement change.

How does culture manifest itself?

Modes of dress (informal, dark suits in the City, less formal suits elsewhere, company uniform)

Attitudes (helpful, couldn't care less, aggressive)

Styles of office/layout (marble banking halls, pristine clear desks, piles of paper, open plan)

Types of buildings (modern, old fashioned, expensive, poorly maintained)

Types of employees (graduates, manual workers, trendy left wing, scientists)

Style of working (clocking on, long hours, extensive travel, etc)

変革总动员

为什么要关注文化？

了解一个企业的文化对于了解怎样最有效地实施变革是十分重要的。

文化是怎样自我表现的？

服装式样(非正式的、在伦敦城中穿着黑色的西装、在别处穿着不那么正式的套装、工作装)

态度(乐于帮忙的、事必躬亲的、积极进取的)

办公室/陈列物的风格(大理石的银行大厅、古朴而整洁的办公桌、成堆的文件、公开的计划)

建筑类型(现代的、旧式的、造价高的、缺乏维护的)

员工类型(大学毕业生、手工工作者、左翼倾向的时髦人物、科学家)

工作方式(计时的、长时间的、长途旅行等)

KEY ELEMENTS OF CULTURE

The key elements that influence culture include:

History (long established, new, product of mergers and acquisitions)

Ownership (entrepreneurial, partnership, institution, State, many small shareholders, family, co-operative)

Operating environment (global, national, regional, local)

Mission (profit, charity, growth, loss leader, quality, mutuality)

People (graduates, manual workers, multi-national, accountants, actuaries, salesmen)

Management style (paternal, hire and fire, benevolent, despotic, sharing, controlling)

IT (how relevant is Information Technology to the industry - farming versus telecoms?)

文化的关键要素

影响文化的关键要素包括：

历史(长久以来形成的、崭新的、合并和收购的产物)

所有权(中间商的、合伙企业的、社会事业机构的、国有的、一些小股东的、家庭的、合作式的)

经营环境(全球的、国内的、区域性的、当地的)

任务(利润、慈善捐款、经济增长、精减领导层、质量、关系)

人员(大学毕业生、手工工作者、多国的、会计师、书记、销售人员)

管理风格(家长式的、雇佣和辞退、慈善的、专制的、分担式的、支配式的)

信息技术(信息技术与工业的相关程度如何——农业与电信业的相关程度又如何?)

CULTURAL AWARENESS

It is the blend of these key elements that makes up the culture of an organisation and in return may also reflect the culture. The culture must therefore be analysed and understood to enable the change programme to be targeted and to be successful in implementation.

Failure to take culture into account will result in just that - failure! - no matter how well planned or executed a change may be.

文化意识

这些关键要素的组合构成了一家企业的文化并且相应地也可能反映着这种文化。因而要使变革计划成为目标并且成功实施,这种文化必须得到分析和理解。

> 不对文化加以考虑只能导致——失败! ——不管变革设计得多么周密或者实施得多么顺利。

TYPES OF CULTURE

Charles Handy in his book `Understanding Organizations' identifies four main types of organisational culture:

Power

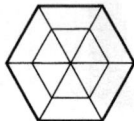

Role

Task

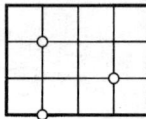

Person

查尔斯·汉迪在他的《理解企业》一书中提出企业文化的四种主要类型：

权力　　　　　　　责任　　　　　　　　任务　　　　　　　　人

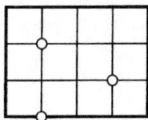

TYPES OF CULTURE

Power

This is symbolised by a web, as power flows along the lines to the centre, rather like the vibrations in a spider's web.

Power is wielded by individuals at the centre (eg: well-established entrepreneurial companies or a political party); decisions are easy but may not be right.

Key levers

To change the organisation, you must get the support of the central authority.

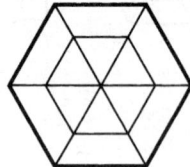

文化类型

权力

这可以用一张网来形象地表示,因为权力沿着线条流向中心,与蜘蛛网里的震动的传播非常相似。

权力为处于中心的成员所支配(例如:已站稳脚跟的中间商公司或是一个政党);决议是轻而易举的但却可能并不正确。

关键杠杆

要改变这种企业,你必须得到中心权力的支持。

TYPES OF CULTURE

Role

This is symbolised by a Greek temple, because it is based on functions and is a very common type where communication flows up (in varying degrees) but never or seldom across (bureaucracy).

Stability is the key and when this goes it falls down, rather like a temple in an earthquake; many organisations fit here.

Key levers

To change this organisation, you must work up each `leg' of the temple, following the structure and protocol. This is not easy and is time consuming. However, it is easier if you have a management structure looking down and across the organisation.

文化类型

责任

这可以用一座希腊神庙来形象地表示,因为它以功能为基础,是一种非常普遍的类型,在那里信息向上传送(以不同的程度)但却从未或者很少通过(官僚组织)。

稳定是关键,失去稳定它就会像地震中的一座神庙那样轰然倒下;许多企业正是这种类型。

关键杠杆

要改变这种企业,你必须依据结构和草图挪动神庙的每一条"腿"。这并不容易而且要花费时间。尽管如此,如果你拥有一份管理结构图来俯视和透视这个企业的话,变革就会容易许多。

TYPES OF CULTURE

Task

This is symbolised by a net, as power flows up, across and down in a matrix structure.

Jobs are project or task oriented and very flexible with no structure.

Consultancies and some innovative companies are like this; a key feature is customer focused objectives.

Key levers

To change this organisation, you must take the key decision makers with you and gain buy-in from most members.

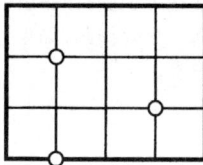

文化类型

任务

这可以用一幅网络来形象地表示,正如权力在一个矩阵结构中向上、向下以及交叉流动一样。

工作就是定向的工程或者任务,非常灵活而没有结构。

顾问医师的工作和一些革新的公司与此相似;一个重要的特色是目标以顾客为中心。

关键杠杆

要改变这种企业,你必须使得重要决策的制定者与你同在并且得到大多数成员的支持。

TYPES OF CULTURE

Person

This is symbolised by a cluster or constellation, as individuals are important. Such an organisation is rare and difficult to manage. Some partnerships are like this and professors within academia also fit this profile, getting on with their own interests, taking time out to meet organisational needs.

Key levers

To change this organisation, you must effectively take everyone with you.

文化类型

人

这可以用一簇花朵或是一个星群来形象地表示,因为个体是重要的。这样一种企业少见而难于管理。一些合伙企业与之相似,学术界里的一些教授也适宜于这种类型,他们一边干着自己的事情,一边抽出时间来满足企业的需要。

关键杠杆

要改变这种企业,你必须有效地获取每一个人的支持。

CULTURE: ORGANISATIONAL ANALYSIS

YES!

Describe below the main symbols that reflect the culture of your organisation in terms of:

Modes of dress _____

Attitudes _____

Style of office _____

Buildings _____

Employees _____

Style of working _____

_____

変革总动员
文化：企业分析

YES!

从以下几个方面描述一下反映你的企业文化的主要标志：

服装式样 _____

态　　度 _____

办公室的设计风格 _____

建筑类型 _____

员工类型 _____

工作方式 _____

99

CULTURE: ORGANISATIONAL ANALYSIS

YES!

Then analyse your organisation and decide which one of the four cultural examples best fits:

		✔
Power		
Role		
Task		
Person		

This will enable you to understand the **key levers** that will need to be moved if undertaking change. NB: This is a simple illustrative exercise, and more detailed analysis is necessary in a full change programme.

文化：企业分析

然后分析你的企业并从四种文化样本中找出最适合的一种：

		✔
权力		
责任		
任务		
人		

这将使你了解了实施变革所需要移动的**关键杠杆**。注意：这只是一次简单的说明性的运用，在一份完整的变革计划中还需要更加详尽的分析。

PEOPLE

HOW THEY REACT

- People react differently to change depending on their own persona, circumstances and understanding of the process

- Those opposed to change obviously need attention, but...

- Even those in favour of change will be affected and need to be managed properly

员工

他们怎样反应

- 员工根据自身的角色、环境和对过程的理解对变革作出不同的反应
- 对那些明确反对变革的人需要加以注意,但是……
- 即便那是赞同变革的人也会受到影响因而需要恰当的管理

PREPARING FOR CHANGE

PEOPLE

NEGATIVE RESPONSE

Why do people have a negative response to change?

- They cannot see the point of the change (eg: the old guard who have been there for a long time)

- They are too busy (shooting the alligators to help in draining the swamp)

- They are threatened by the change (directly/indirectly)

- They <u>perceive</u> that they are threatened by the change

- Their politics make them natural enemies of the change

- There are cultural problems

Part of change management is identifying these problems and planning to negate them or obviate them.

员工
消极态度

员工为什么会对变革采取一种消极反应?

- 他们没有看到变革的主旨(例如:那些在职时间很久的老的卫护者)
- 他们非常繁忙(射杀鳄鱼以助于排干沼泽)
- 他们受到变革的威胁(直接/间接)
- 他们认为他们会受到变革的威胁
- 他们的政见使他们成为变革天然的敌人
- 存在文化上的问题

变革管理的一部分就是分清这些问题并且指定计划来消除或者避免它们。

PEOPLE

NEGATIVE RESPONSE

A negative response to change is to be expected. Change is different and many people will be against it on principle, whatever it actually means for them.

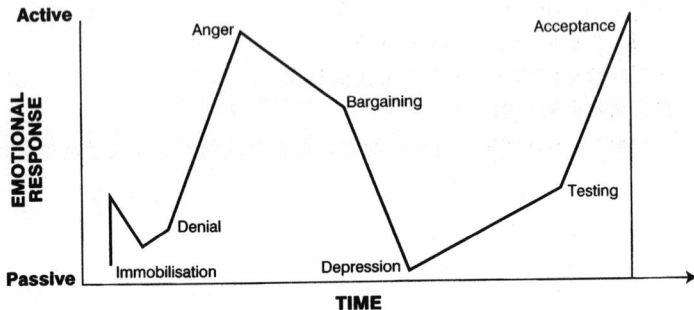

变革总动员

员工

消极态度

对变革的消极态度是意料之中的。变革意味着不同并且许多人将会在原则上反对它，无论变革对于他们确切意味着什么。

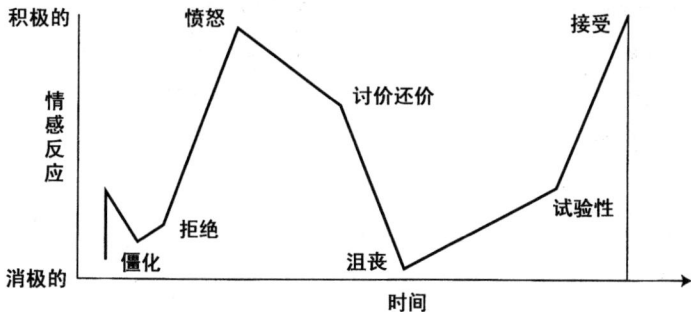

图中纵轴为"情感反应"，从"消极的"到"积极的"；横轴为"时间"。曲线依次标注：僵化、拒绝、愤怒、讨价还价、沮丧、试验性、接受。

PREPARING FOR CHANGE

PEOPLE
NEGATIVE RESPONSE

A negative response to change is similar to grieving for the loss of a loved one. The difference may be in the timing and the difficulty of accepting the change; but the emotional responses are the same, requiring **step-handling** to meet each of the changing emotions:

- Immobilisation
- Denial
- Anger
- Bargaining

- Depression
- Testing
- Acceptance

变革总动员

员工
消极态度

    对待变革的负面反应类似于失去一个爱人的伤痛。差别可能就在于接受改变的时间以及难度;但是情感的反应是同样的,在面临每一种变化着的感情时都需要**逐步地应付**:

- 僵化
- 拒绝
- 愤怒
- 讨价还价
- 沮丧
- 尝试
- 接受

PEOPLE
POSITIVE RESPONSE

Even those in favour of the change - such as those starting a new job, those about to be married, those moving home and (NB: change managers) those on secondment to projects - will need managing to ensure that they do not succumb to pessimism as they move through the different phases.

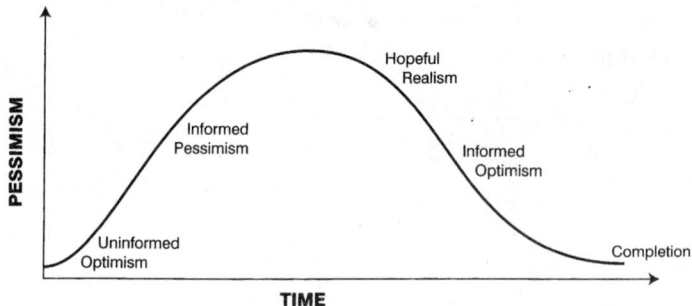

变革总动员

员工

积极态度

即便那些赞同变革的人——例如那些开始一份新的工作的人,那些将要结婚的人,那些移动的家庭和(注意:变革管理人)那些借调到计划中来的人——将需要管理以确保他们在通过不同的阶段时不会屈从于悲观主义。

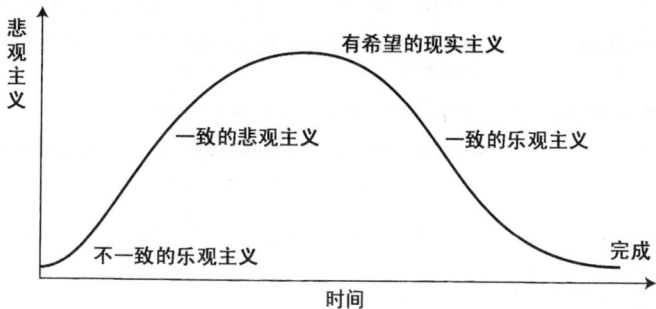

PEOPLE

POSITIVE RESPONSE

Reactions will be different at each phase of the change programme:

Uninformed optimism: People are self-confident and positive towards the change

Informed pessimism: People start exhibiting negative responses to change; lose confidence

Hopeful realism: People start to see achievability of change; confidence starts growing

Informed optimism: Confidence returns; people throw themselves into project

Completion: People help rest of organisation; give out confidence

员工
积极态度

在变革计划的每一个阶段反应都会有所不同:

不一致的乐观主义: 员工对变革自信而乐观

一致的悲观主义: 员工开始表现出对待变革的消极态度;丧失信心

有希望的现实主义: 员工开始看到变革的曙光;信心开始增长

一致的乐观主义: 信心恢复;员工全身心投入计划之中

完成: 员工促成企业的安定;散发着信心

ORGANISATIONAL READINESS TO CHANGE

- Change is difficult; before starting a change programme, it makes sense to assess just how difficult it will be to push through

- The culture of an organisation will affect the ability and speed of an organisation to accept change because it is a way of life

- To change an organisation you must change the people, their beliefs and attitudes and their ways of working; this can be very difficult, especially in strong cultures and often in successful companies (no burning platform)

- It is, therefore, important to understand the readiness of the organisation and management to change

通往变革的企业准备

- 变革是艰难的;在开展一项变革计划前,对推进它的难度做出评估是很有意义的
- 一家企业的文化将会影响到一家企业接受变革的能力和速度,因为文化是一种生活的方式
- 要改变一家企业你就必须改变那些员工,他们的信仰、态度以及他们工作的方式;这会是艰难的,特别是在强有力的文化以及成功的企业之中(没有燃烧平台)
- 因而弄清企业通往变革的准备以及管理方式是十分重要的

PREPARING FOR CHANGE

ORGANISATIONAL READINESS TO CHANGE

MEASUREMENT

	Organisational change style	
Low	Proactive	Reactive
High	Average	Static

ENVIRONMENTAL STABILITY (vertical axis: Low at top, High at bottom)

High ————————————————— Low

MANAGEMENT ADAPTABILITY TO CHANGE

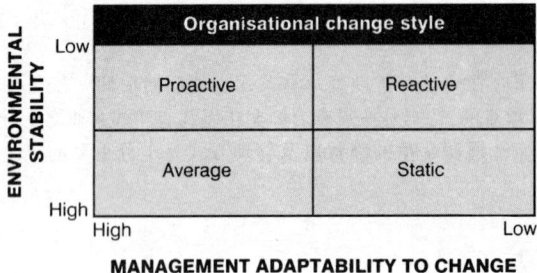

(Based on the work of Harvey and Brown)

116

변革总动员
通往变革的企业准备
衡量

	企业的变革类型	
超 前 式		应 激 式
普 通 式		静 态 式

环境稳固性: 低 → 高

对变革的管理适应性: 高 ←→ 低

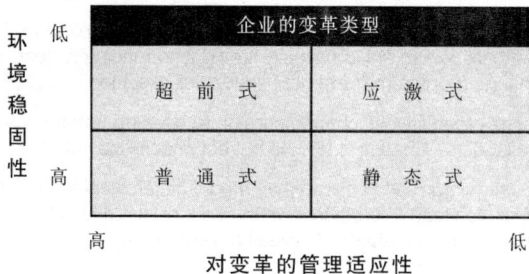

(根据哈维和布朗的著作)

ORGANISATIONAL READINESS TO CHANGE

YES!

Proactive: These organisations have dynamic management within unstable environments and need to keep one step ahead of the game; change is a way of life for them.

Reactive: These change only when they have to - usually in response to step change in competition and are continually fire-fighting/running to keep still. Change programmes are not usually well executed.

Average: These organisations change enough to keep up with the market - but behind the leaders. Change is difficult but not impossible. Most organisations fit here.

Static: A static organisation usually has a rigid hierarchical style of management which can lead to problems when suddenly the rules of the game change. Change here is extremely difficult to push through.

变革总动员

通往变革的企业准备

超前式：这些企业在变化的环境中采取动态的管理并且想要在行业中领先一步；变革是他们生存的方式。

应激式：仅仅在他们别无选择的时候——通常是在竞争中做出响应而采取变革，而且总是要持续作战/不停奔跑以保持稳定。
变革计划通常没有彻底地执行。

普通式：这些企业改变得足以跟上市场——但是落后于先行者们。变革是困难的但并非没有可能。大多数企业属于此类。

静态式：一家静态式的企业通常具有一种严格的阶级式的管理风格，在游戏规则突然改变时便会引起问题。在这里推行变革是极其艰难的。

PREPARING FOR CHANGE

CASE STUDY 1
QUESTION

A major change programme is about to be initiated in a company. What would be the key steps to be taken up to the announcement?

_____

_____

_____

_____

_____

_____

_____

ANSWER →

案例研究 1

问题

YES!

一项重要的变革计划即将在一家公司展开。发布通告主要应采取哪些步骤？

答案 →

PREPARING FOR CHANGE

CASE STUDY 1
ANSWER

The steps would include:

- Prepare a communications plan

- Develop questions and answers for top level managers to use when briefing their staff

- Inform major stakeholders

- Brief top level managers and inform them of the timing of the cascade of information down the layers of the organisation

- Issue press release (if appropriate)

- Issue communication to everyone

变革总动员

案例研究 1

答案

步骤包括:

- 准备一份沟通方案
- 为最高管理层详述问题及其解答以便他们用来向其职员介绍基本情况
- 通知主要的股东
- 向最高管理层介绍基本情况并且告知他们信息在企业内逐层传递的时间安排
- 发布新闻稿(如果合适的话)
- 发出写给每个员工的信

PREPARING FOR CHANGE

CASE STUDY 2

QUESTION

An employee has just been seconded to a change programme from his normal job. List below the emotions he might have when he is told, and then describe how to handle them.

_____

_____

_____

How I would handle his emotions: _____

_____

_____

_____

_____

ANSWER ⟶

変革总动员

案例研究 2

问题

一位员工刚刚从他日常的工作岗位临时调往一项变革计划。在下面列出他得知这一消息后可能会有的情绪,然后描述一下如何应对。

_____

_____

_____

我会怎样应对他的情绪:

_____

_____

_____

答案 ➝

PREPARING FOR CHANGE

CASE STUDY 2
ANSWER

The person's reaction to change will be:

- Elation at being chosen coupled with fear for the future post-project

- Concern at the responsibility

- Anxiety about his current reporting relationships

- Lack of certainty regarding his role

- Possible worries about his ability

These concerns can be handled by his current superior giving him a proper briefing and explaining that the secondment represents a vote of confidence in him and his abilities, and by stressing the importance of the project and the role. This would then be followed by a subsequent briefing from the project director along similar lines but in more detail.

那个员工对调动的反应会是:

- 被选中的兴高采烈中掺杂着对方案之后的前途的担忧
- 关注职责
- 对他目前的从属关系的担忧
- 对他的任务缺乏了解
- 可能会有的对他自身能力的担忧

这些担忧可以通过他目前的上级向他做出适当的情况简介、向他解释暂时的调动意味着对他以及他的能力的信任、强调方案以及任务的重要性来应对。之后可以由方案责任人沿相似但更加详尽的思路阐明情况。

CASE STUDY 3

QUESTION

A company has just been acquired. What must the new owners do to ensure a smooth transition period?

_____

_____

_____

_____

_____

_____

_____

ANSWER →

案例研究 3

问题

YES!

一家公司刚刚被收购。新的所有者要确保一段平稳的过渡期必须做些什么？

_____

_____

_____

_____

_____

_____

_____

答案 ➔ (129)

CASE STUDY 3
ANSWER

The acquiring company must immediately issue a communication to all staff setting out the blueprint for the future, ensuring that change is kept aligned with the present culture as much as possible. Specifically the company should:

- Explain any immediate changes to operations

- Set out the longer-term plans

- Stress the benefits that are expected to accrue from the acquisition

- Set up briefing meetings and a channel for communications

- Ensure that concerns are met and dealt with sympathetically (the acquisition of Barings Bank where the bonus was maintained is a very good example of this)

案例研究 3

答案

YES!

　　该收购公司必须立即发出写给全体员工的信以陈述对于未来的蓝图，并确保变革与目前的文化尽可能地一致。这家公司尤其应该：

- 解释任何与企业经营直接相关的改变
- 陈述较长时期的方案
- 强调可以从收购中获得的预期收益
- 设立基本情况介绍会和沟通渠道
- 确保所有的关注都被触及并且得到耐心的处理（一个很好的例子就是被收购的巴林银行中奖金继续保留）

MAKING CHANGE HAPPEN

成功实施变革

KEY STEPS

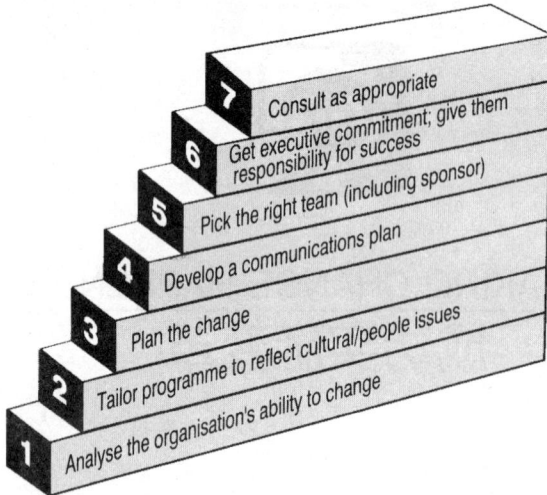

7 Consult as appropriate

6 Get executive commitment; give them responsibility for success

5 Pick the right team (including sponsor)

4 Develop a communications plan

3 Plan the change

2 Tailor programme to reflect cultural/people issues

1 Analyse the organisation's ability to change

关键步骤

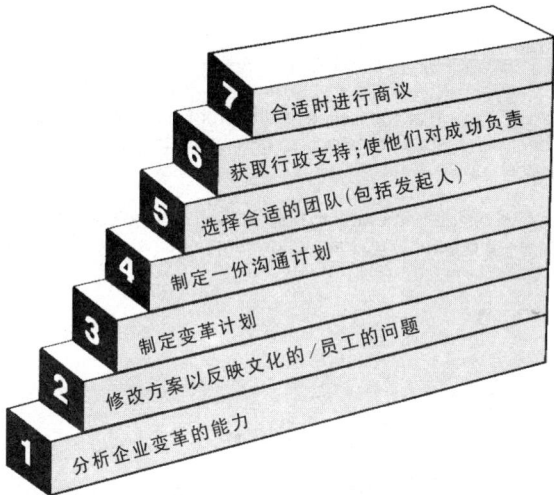

7 合适时进行商议

6 获取行政支持;使他们对成功负责

5 选择合适的团队(包括发起人)

4 制定一份沟通计划

3 制定变革计划

2 修改方案以反映文化的/员工的问题

1 分析企业变革的能力

CHANGE MANAGEMENT FRAMEWORK

The key to successful change management is planning.

Planning means thinking through all the issues, all the problems that you might encounter, the steps necessary to deal with them and the choice of team that will be required. If this means getting external help, then do so.

In the following pages we offer a framework to help you in planning your change programme. This can be used for any programme no matter how large or small - the difference will be the extent of the resources and the complexity of the change.

成功实施变革

变革管理框架

　　制定计划是成功管理变革的关键。

　　制定计划意味着对所有你可能遇到的争议和问题、应对它们的必要步骤以及选择所需团队加以考虑。如果这意味着获得外部帮助，那么就去谋求。

　　在接下来的几页中我们提供了一幅框架来帮助你策划你的变革方案。无论方案规模大小它都适用——差别只在于资源的范围以及变革的复杂程度。

CHANGE MANAGEMENT FRAMEWORK

This table sets out the key tasks, methods and outputs for a change management programme.

	OBJECTIVES >	TASKS >	METHODS >	OUTPUTS
Analysis (Phase I)	to understand the organisation, its culture and the capacity for change	review: structure, strategy, culture, systems, morale, management practices, external environment	desk research, interviews, workshops, brainstorming	organisational analysis, culture "map", change capacity
Design (Phase II)	to agree the vision, build the team and obtain consensus	develop vision, select team, build buy-in	workshops, meetings, communications	vision, team, consensus, leader/support

Table continued opposite ➝

138

变革管理框架

这张图表列出一份变革管理方案的关键任务、方法与产物。

	目　标	任　务	方　法	输　出
分析 (阶段 1)	了解这家企业，它的文化以及变革的能力	审核： 结构,战略, 文化,系统, 士气,管理策略, 外部环境	伏案研究, 访问, 研讨会, 集体自由讨论	企业分析结果, 文化图解, 变革能力
设计 (阶段 2)	赞同远景，构造团队以及达成一致	发展远景, 挑选团队, 构筑买进	研讨会, 集会, 沟通	远景, 团队, 一致, 领导者/支持

图表在对面继续 ➡

CHANGE MANAGEMENT FRAMEWORK

	OBJECTIVES	TASKS	METHODS	OUTPUTS
Planning (Phase III)	to plan the realisation of the change	develop plan, build in contingencies, allocate resources, agree timing	desk research, field research, workshops, planning methodologies	plan, risk analysis, dependency chart, agreed resources
Implementation (Phase IV)	to realise the vision by putting the change(s) through the organisation	roll out change across the organisation, communicate to stakeholders, manage risks and dependencies	meetings, actions, team work, workshops, communications	changed organisation, improved performance, survival, changed culture

(140)

变革管理框架

	目标	任务	方法	输出
计划 (阶段3)	为变革的实现制定计划	发展计划，纳入偶然性，分配资源，对时间安排达成一致	伏案研究，实地调查，研讨会，计划的方法论	计划，风险分析，附属图表，赞同的力量
执行 (阶段4)	在企业内部推行变革以实现远景	在企业内展开变革，与赌金持有者沟通，管理风险以及附属事物	集会，行动，团队工作，研讨会，沟通	变革后的企业，提高的业绩，继续生存，变革后的文化

CHANGE MANAGEMENT FRAMEWORK

Phase I - Analysis

- In this phase it is necessary to understand both the nature of the change and the organisation's culture and its capacity for change

- This will involve carrying out surveys of staff and past projects, and reviewing the structure, strategy, management styles and how the firm interacts with the external environment

Output

- The output from this phase is an understanding of the organisation as it relates to the project and a `map' of the culture

- This should enable you to plan to avoid the potential pitfalls which could arise in the next phase

- Having assessed the change capacity, the pace and scale of change can be optimised

变革管理框架

阶段 1——分析

- 在这个阶段里,了解变革的本质、企业文化以及变革能力是十分必要的
- 这包括开展对全体职员和以往项目的调查,审核结构、战略、管理风格以及公司与外界环境的互动

输出

- 这个阶段的产物是当企业与项目和文化图景相连时对于它的理解
- 这能使你为避开下一个阶段中的潜在危险做出计划
- 对变革能力做出评估之后,变革的节奏和规模就能够得到优化

CHANGE MANAGEMENT FRAMEWORK

Phase II - Design

- In this phase of the project the programme is designed; this should be undertaken at a high level and will involve agreeing the precise nature of the vision, building the team to implement the changes and starting to get buy-in from personnel

- The champion should also be agreed at this stage prior to detailed planning; communication, workshops and discussions are critical at this point

Output

- Includes shared vision, team building and agreed responsibilities

变革管理框架

阶段 2——设计

- 在项目的这个阶段设计方案;这应该在一个较高的层面进行并且应该与远景的准确特征相吻合,构建团队来执行变革并且开始谋求全体员工的支持
- 在做出详细计划之前,拥护者在这个阶段也应该达成共识;在这一点上,沟通、研讨会议和商议都是至关重要的

输出

- 包括普遍认同的远景、团队建设以及一致的职责

CHANGE MANAGEMENT FRAMEWORK

Phase III - Planning

- The objective here is to plan the realisation of the change; this requires looking to the future and thinking through all the risks, dependencies, contingencies and potential problems, and putting together a plan to address them all

- This would include allocating resources, agreeing timing, analysing implications and obtaining buy-in in principle from those affected by talking to them and getting their input

Output

- Will include plans, risk analysis, dependency chart and resources to achieve the plan

阶段 3——计划

- 这里的目标是要设计变革的实现。这需要展望未来并且彻底考虑所有的风险、附属事物、偶然性与潜在的问题,针对它们整理出一个计划
- 这可能会包括分配资源、商定日程安排、分析牵连关系并且通过与受变革影响的员工进行交谈得到信息从而在原则上获得他们的支持

输出

- 包括计划、风险分析、附属图表以及为实现计划所需的资源

CHANGE MANAGEMENT FRAMEWORK

Phase IV - Implementation

- Having put the plan together you must now implement it

- This means ensuring that the plan is followed and that it is re-evaluated in the light of changes to the operating environment and/or strategy and because things crop up which were not foreseen

- The critical skills here are project management and diplomacy, better management of the previous stages will make this stage that much easier

Output

- A well-managed and successful change programme

变革管理框架

阶段 4——执行

- 整理好计划之后,你现在必须执行它了
- 这意味着要确保计划被跟踪并且根据操作环境和/或战略的变更而重新评估,因为没有预料到的事物会突然出现
- 这里的关键技能在于项目的管理手段和圆熟;前面阶段管理得当将使这一阶段的执行更加简易

输出

- 一个管理完备的成功的变革方案

MAKING CHANGE HAPPEN

IMPLEMENTATION PLAN

PROJECT	JUN	JUL	AUG	SEP	OCT	NOV	DEC	JAN	FEB	MAR	APR	MAY
MOBILISATION												
CHANGE MANAGEMENT (Change management line expanded to demonstrate some key activities)												
Agree communication strategy												
Issue communications												
Agree team												
Hold initial briefing meetings												
Hold workshops												
Re-evaluate change plan												
Make changes and re-brief as necessary												
INFORMATION TECHNOLOGY												
RESTRUCTURE TREASURY												
GL / MIS / BUDGETING												
PROCESS IMPROVEMENTS												
DISTRIBUTION CHANNELS												
"HOUSEKEEPING"												
RE-ENGINEER NEW PRODUCT DEVELOPMENT												
MARKETING												
PROGRESS MEETINGS	☆	☆	☆	☆	☆	☆	☆	☆	☆	☆	☆	☆

(150)

实施计划

项　　目	6月	7月	8月	9月	10月	11月	12月	1月	2月	3月	4月	5月
动　员	■											
变革管理(扩展变革管理线以示范一些关键活动)	■	■	■	■	■	■	■	■	■	■	■	■
认同沟通策略	■											
进行沟通	■		■		■		■		■		■	
认同团队	■											
召开初步情况介绍会		■		■		■	■					
召开研讨会议			■									
重新评估变革计划							■					
促进变革,必要时再次作简要介绍								■		■		■
信息技术	■	■	■	■	■		■	■		■	■	■
资金重组	■	■	■									
GL/管理信息系统/预算	■	■	■	■				■				
过程改进			■	■	■	■			■	■		
分配渠道				■	■		■	■				
"家政"			■		■	■						
重新设计新产品的发展						■	■					
市　场											■	
进展会议	☆	☆	☆	☆	☆	☆	☆	☆	☆	☆	☆	☆

(151)

IMPLEMENTATION PLAN

The chart opposite shows how change management fits in with a programme and how it is supportive of the larger goals.

Such goals may be to implement: a new IT infrastructure; a radically new organisation; redesigned process; etc.

Whatever the change, it is necessary to integrate the change management into the overall programme.

实施计划

 对面的表格显示了变革管理是如何与一个方案相适应以及怎样支持更大的目标。

 这些目标可能是去建构：一项新的信息技术基础；一个崭新的企业；重新设计的过程等等。

 无论是哪种变革，都必须将变革管理纳入到整个方案之中。

MAKING CHANGE HAPPEN

COMMITMENT

	Resistance (active)	Let it happen (passive)	Help it happen	Make it happen
Make it happen	3	4	5	5
Help it happen	2	3	4	5
Let it happen (passive)	1	2	3	4
Resistance (active)	1	1	2	3

EXECUTIVE COMMITMENT (vertical axis)

STAFF COMMITMENT (horizontal axis)

INCREASING CHANCE OF SUCCESS

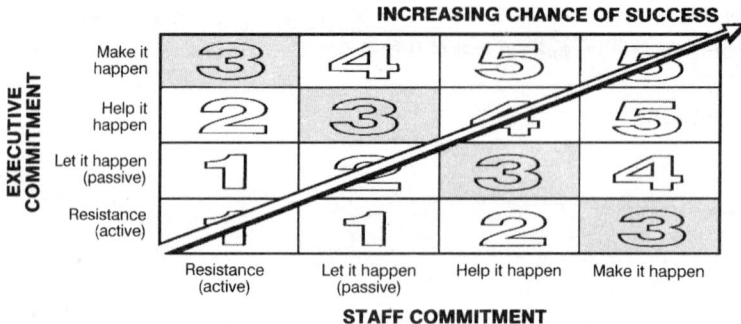

2 or below : forget   4 or above : success   3 : needs work

Successful project management moves the project from the bottom left to the top right.

154

成功实施变革
承诺

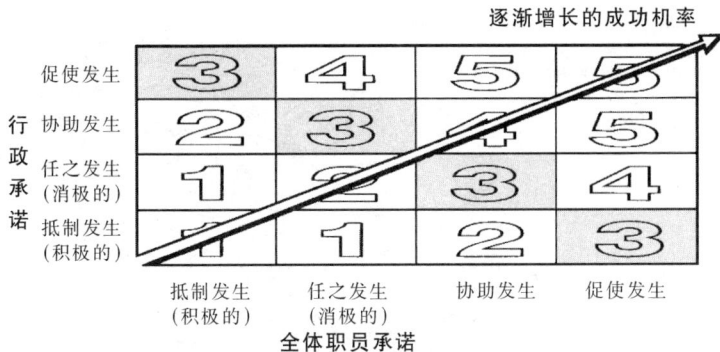

逐渐增长的成功机率

行政承诺	抵制发生（积极的）	任之发生（消极的）	协助发生	促使发生
促使发生	3	4	5	5
协助发生	2	3	4	5
任之发生（消极的）	1	2	3	4
抵制发生（积极的）	1	1	2	3

全体职员承诺

2 或其以下：忽视   **4** 或其以上：成功   **3** 需要工作

成功的项目管理引导项目从左下向右上移动。

155

TEAM MANAGEMENT

A small dedicated team to manage change can have a major effect on an organisation, one which is disproportionate to the size of the team. Selecting the right individuals is, therefore, critical.

团队管理

　　一个小的管理变革的专职团队能够给企业带来巨大的与团队规模不成正比的效用。因此选择合适的成员至关重要。

TEAM MANAGEMENT
ROLES

A number of roles are critical to successful change management. Select the right people or the project will fail. Team numbers will vary depending on project size and duration.

- A senior executive must visibly sponsor the project
- A senior person must take day-to-day responsibility
- A full-time project manager with experience of managing change must run the project (often a role for external consultants)
- Include people with knowledge of the organisation and experience of change programmes (external consultants often involved too)
- Sufficient people at all levels in the organisation must be ambassadors of progress to help spread the word
- Outside consultants can often act as useful catalysts because of their independence

Test proposed team members for appropriateness using some of the many methods available (Belbin, 16PF, Myers-Briggs, ODR, etc). This ensures the correct blend of skills.

成功实施变革
团队管理
责任

　　众多责任对于成功的变革管理是非常重要的。选择合适的员工否则项目便会失败。团队成员的数量取决于项目的规模以及持续时间。
- 一位高级执行者必须明确地支持这个项目
- 一位高级员工必须承担起日常职责
- 一位全职的有管理变革经验的项目管理者必须运转这个项目(常常是为外界顾问准备的角色)
- 接纳了解企业和拥有变革方案经验的员工(常常也包括外界顾问)
- 在企业内部各个层面保证充足的人员作为方案的代言人来协助传播消息
- 因为独立性,外界顾问经常可以充当有益的催化剂

　　使用一些已有方式(Belbin, 16PF, Myers-Briggs, ODR, 等等)测试被推荐的团队成员适宜与否。这样可以确保技能的正确融合。

MAKING CHANGE HAPPEN

TEAM MANAGEMENT
DEVELOPMENT PROCESS

TEAMS

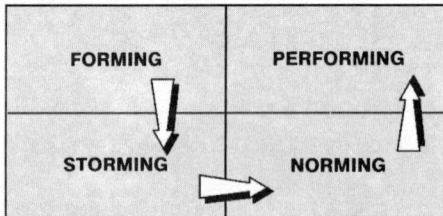

Team members do not usually work well together from day one and have to go through a development process of finding out about each other and achieving a working understanding. Only then will they deliver. The earlier teams form, the quicker they move into productive performance.

团　　队

形　成　期	履　行　期
困　扰　期	规　范　期

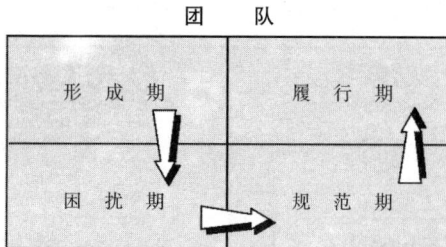

　　团队成员通常并不能从一开始就在一起协调工作，因而不得不通过一个发展过程来互相认识以达成工作上的理解。只有那时他们才能够履行职责。团队形成得越早，他们创造经济价值的速度也就越快。

TEAM MANAGEMENT
DEVELOPMENT PROCESS

The four development stages that teams go through are generally recognised as follows:

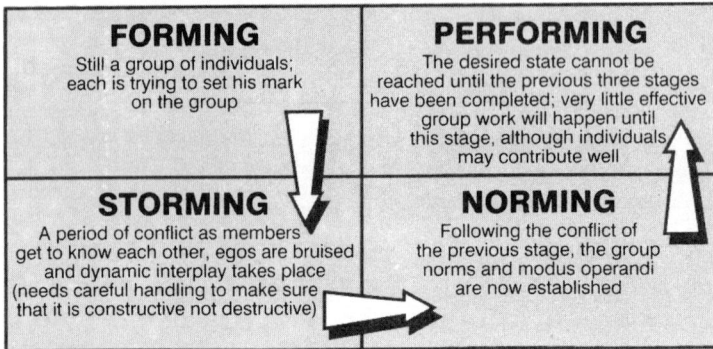

FORMING	PERFORMING
Still a group of individuals; each is trying to set his mark on the group	The desired state cannot be reached until the previous three stages have been completed; very little effective group work will happen until this stage, although individuals may contribute well
STORMING	NORMING
A period of conflict as members get to know each other, egos are bruised and dynamic interplay takes place (needs careful handling to make sure that it is constructive not destructive)	Following the conflict of the previous stage, the group norms and modus operandi are now established

成功实施变革

团队管理

发展过程

团队形成的四个发展阶段通常被认为如下所示：

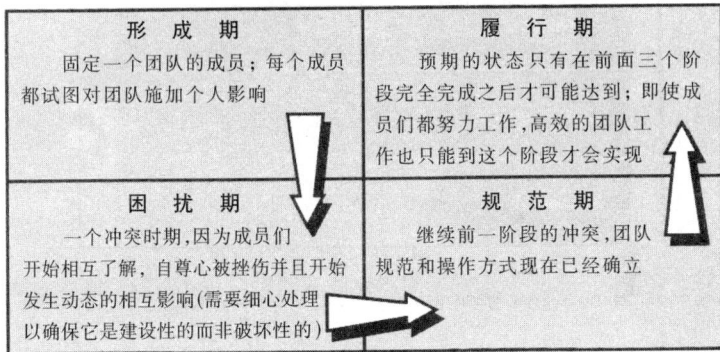

形 成 期	履 行 期
固定一个团队的成员；每个成员都试图对团队施加个人影响	预期的状态只有在前面三个阶段完全完成之后才可能达到；即使成员们都努力工作，高效的团队工作也只能到这个阶段才会实现
困 扰 期	规 范 期
一个冲突时期，因为成员们开始相互了解，自尊心被挫伤并且开始发生动态的相互影响(需要细心处理以确保它是建设性的而非破坏性的)	继续前一阶段的冲突，团队规范和操作方式现在已经确立

REACTIONS TO CHANGE

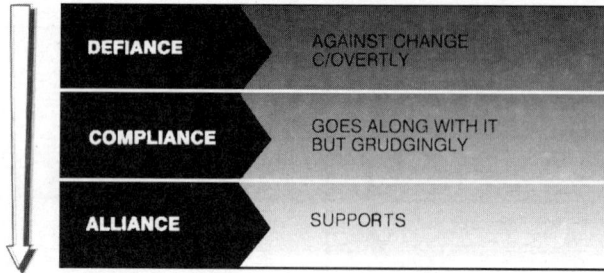

DEFIANCE	AGAINST CHANGE C/OVERTLY
COMPLIANCE	GOES ALONG WITH IT BUT GRUDGINGLY
ALLIANCE	SUPPORTS

The challenge is to move the organisation and people down the scale.

变革反应

对　抗	公然/偷偷摸摸地对抗变革
顺　从	赞同变革,然而勉强
联　盟	支持

挑战在于将企业和员工沿着等级向下移动。

RESISTANCE

When you come to implement the changes, no matter what you have done to prepare the ground, it will still come as a surprise to many people.

This surprise will turn into resistance quickly and must be managed to ensure success.

Address people's fears to gain their commitment.

阻力

　　当你开始实施变革,无论你做过多少准备工作,对一些员工而言变革还是会作为一个意外而出现。

　　这种意外很快会导致阻力因而必须加以管理以确保成功。

　　关注员工的担忧以获取他们的支持。

MAKING CHANGE HAPPEN

RESISTANCE

Resistance is a vote for the status quo and must be dealt with to prevent disruptive behaviour. It must be planned for and handled well, otherwise it will get worse and could damage the project.

> Corporate America is littered with the wreckage of technically sound programs that have been crushed by employee resistance to change
>
> *Tom Terez, Modern Management*

阻力

抵制变革是对现存状态的支持和赞同,因而必须妥善处理以避免破坏性行为。它必须被计划在内并得到恰当处理,否则它会变得更糟并可能破坏这个项目。

"整个美国都充斥着技术上合理却因为员工抵制变革而破产的方案残骸"

汤姆·特雷茨,现代管理

MAKING CHANGE HAPPEN

RESISTANCE
REASONS

Resistance occurs for many reasons, both real and supposed:

- Loss of control
- Uncertainty
- Fear of the difference
- Loss of power
- Possible increased workloads
- Threat
- Misunderstandings

A successful change management programme will address these causes and negate them.

成功实施变革

阻力

原因

阻力的出现有很多原因,包括现实的和假定的:

- 失去控制
- 不确定
- 对差异的恐惧
- 权力的丧失
- 可能增加的工作量
- 威胁
- 误解

一个成功的变革管理方案应该关注这些原因并且消除它们。

RESISTANCE
HOW TO DEAL WITH IT

Resistance can be overcome when you:

- Involve people in the process

- Train

- Explain the change in easy to understand terms

- Develop shared vision and buy-in

- Explain the reasons (burning platform)

- Address the concerns of stakeholders

- **Above all, communicate**

阻力

如何应对

阻力可以被克服,当你:

- 让员工参与到过程中来
- 培训
- 以简单的方式解释变革以助于理解术语
- 获取普遍认同的远景和支持
- 解释原因(燃烧平台)
- 关注赌金持有者的担忧
- **最重要的是沟通**

RESISTANCE

GAINING ACCEPTANCE

Gaining acceptance goes through the process below, starting with those who are most likely to accept change - innovators - until finally the laggards are won over - or leave.
Use the innovators as Ambassadors of Progress.

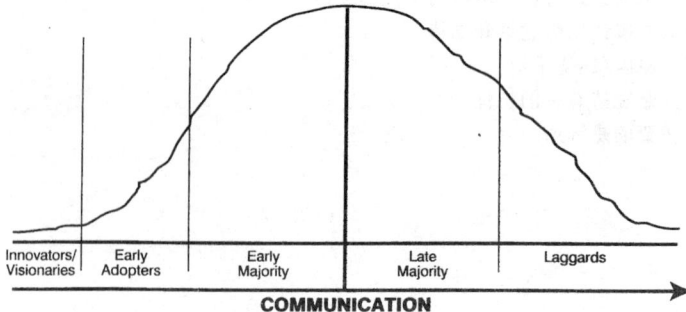

阻力

获取认同

　　获取认同贯穿于下面这个过程，从那些最可能接受变革的员工——革新者——到最后落后者被争取过来——或者离开。

让革新者作为进程的代言人。

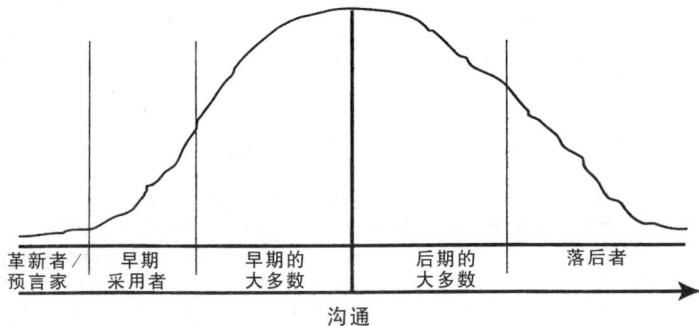

| 革新者/
预言家 | 早期
采用者 | 早期的
大多数 | 后期的
大多数 | 落后者 |

沟通

NOTES
笔 记

COMMUNICATION
沟通面对面

COMMUNICATION

THE FIVE Ws

Who should be told?

When should they be told?

What should they be told?

Where should the message be conveyed?

Who should control the communications process?

Addressing the FIVE Ws is an essential element of a change programme.
Poor communication means that the wrong messages can go out and, therefore,
misunderstandings occur - leading to resistance, antipathy and often failure.

五个 W

谁应该被告知?

他们应该何时被告知?

他们应该被告知些什么?

信息应该被传达到何处?

谁应该控制沟通过程?

对这五个 W 的关注在变革方案中是至关重要的元素。缺乏沟通意味着错误的信息会传播,从而导致误解——引起抵制、反感并且通常会走向失败。

THE FIVE Ws
WHO?

- Everyone who needs to be told about something should be told

- Openness is the key (although there will always be some things which are not disseminated as widely as others)

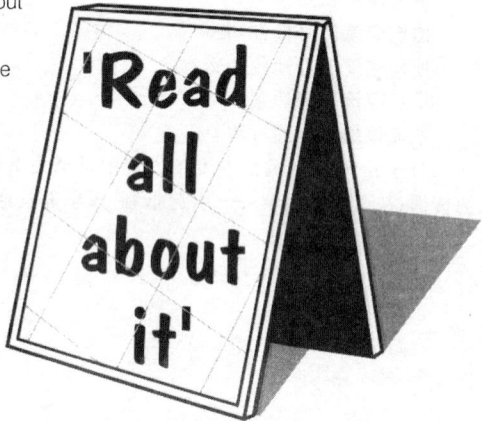

'Read all about it'

五个 W

谁?

- 每一个需要被告知的人都必须被告知
- 保持公开性是关键(尽管总是有些事情传播得不如其他事情广泛)

"阅读 关于 它的 一切"

COMMUNICATION

THE FIVE Ws
WHEN?

- Project members must be briefed prior to them joining the project

- All affected employees should be told at the **same** time, to avoid spread of rumours

- Brief those internally before those externally; you don't want staff finding out about change from the media

- Make an announcement following a significant event or decision

(182)

五个 W

何时?

- 在项目成员加入之前必须向他们简介情况
- 所有相关的雇员必须在同一时间被告知,以避免流言
- 先作内部介绍再作外部宣传;你不会希望职员从媒体中发现变革
- 在重要事件或者决议之后作出通告

THE FIVE Ws
WHAT?

The four rules of communication are:

- Tell `em when you have something to say
- Tell `em what you plan to do
- Tell `em what you are doing
- Tell `em what you will be doing

五个 W

什么?

沟通的四个原则为:

- 告诉他们何时你会有所宣布
- 告诉他们你打算做些什么
- 告诉他们你正在做些什么
- 告诉他们你将来会做些什么

COMMUNICATION

THE FIVE Ws
WHERE?

- Choose the most effective vehicle to get your message across

- This could be via seminars, staff letters, press releases or whatever; the key is to make sure that your message gets across to the right people, to avoid rumours and hearsay

(186)

沟通面对面

五个 W

何处？

- 为你的信息传递选择最有效的传达手段
- 这可以通过研讨会、职员信件、新闻发布会或任何其他方式；关键要确保你的信息传达到合适的人员以避免流言蜚语和道听途说

THE FIVE Ws
WHO SHOULD CONTROL IT?

Usually communications will be under the control of the sponsoring executive.
For a large programme, this is usually the CEO.

It is such an important part of the programme's success that it MUST NOT be left to a junior.

- The project manager will normally have input into it

- Personnel will usually be consulted

- The corporate communications people, if appropriate, will be involved

沟通面对面

五个 W

谁该控制?

沟通通常应该由行政发起人控制。对于一个大型的方案而言,这通常是首席行政长官。

作为方案成功的重要组成部分,变革**不应该**由职位较低者来控制。

- 通常会对沟通有所影响的项目管理者
- 常常会献计献策的员工
- 所有的传播人员,如果合适的话,将被包含在内

NOTES
笔 记

EPILOGUE

后　记

HOW TO SUCCEED

Success in Change Management involves being **SMART**:

Strategy defined

Management buy-in

Assurance to staff

Risk analysis

Time critical implementation

如何成功

变革管理的成功包含着要保持**机灵**：

经过详细说明的战略

管理层的支持

对职员的把握

风险分析

为关键的执行行动选择时机

HOW TO FAIL

Change Management will fail when you are **STUPID:**

Sponsorship not forthcoming

Team members do not function as agents of change

Unclear vision and commitment

Poorly planned change programme

Inappropriate/insufficient communication

Don't take account of culture

如何失败

当你**愚蠢**时变革管理会失败：
赞助没有到来
团队成员没有行使变革代理人的职责
不明朗的远景和承诺
计划不完备的变革方案
不恰当的／不充足的沟通
没有考虑到文化

TIPS

Confrontation

Avoid confrontation; obtain a consensus

Manpower changes

Changes in manpower (which often result from
change) must be dealt with sympathetically
to ensure buy-in and acceptance as well as
good morale for remaining staff

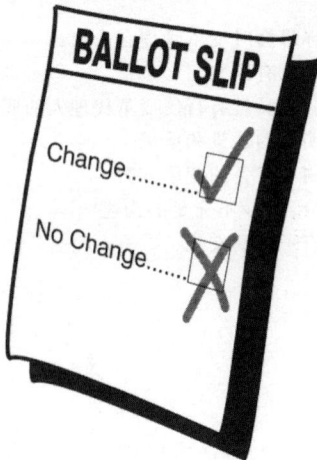

BALLOT SLIP

Change.......... ✓

No Change...... ✗

小技巧

对峙
避免对峙;达成共识
人力资源变革
人力资源的变革（经常作为变革的产物）必须处之以高度的同情心以确保支持与接受以及余留员工的良好士气

TIPS

Automation

Bear in mind that automation usually results in manual positions being made redundant

Co-operation and buy-in

It is important that buy-in is obtained from
staff by consensus and not imposition

小技巧

自动化
切记自动化通常会使手工操作成为多余

合作与支持
以多数通过方式而不是强制方式从职员中获得支持是很重要的

FURTHER READING

`Change Masters', by Rosabeth Moss Kantor, published by Unwin

`Managing at the Speed of Change', by Daryl Connor, published by Villard Books

`The Fifth Discipline', by Peter Senge, published by Century Business

`The Essence of Change', by Liz Clarke, published by Prentice Hall

`An Experiential Approach to Organization Development', by Harvey and Brown, published by Prentice Hall

'Understanding Organizations', by Charles Handy, published by Pelican

'Organizational Transitions', by Beckhard and Harris, published by Addison-Wesley

进阶阅读

《变革大师》，罗莎贝斯·莫斯·坎特著，Unwin 出版

《控制变革的速度》，达里尔·科勒著，Villard Books 出版

《第五项原则》，彼得·桑吉著，Century Business 出版

《变革的要素》，莉兹·克拉克著，Prentice Hall 出版

《组织发展的实验性方案》，哈维和布朗合著，Prentice Hall 出版

《认识组织》，查尔斯·汉迪著，Pelican 出版

《组织变迁》，贝克哈德和哈里斯合著，Addison-Westey 出版

About the Author

Neil Russell-Jones

Neil, an MBA, is a management consultant. He is a chartered banker and a member of the Strategic Planning Society. He has worked internationally with many organisations, particularly in the areas of strategy, BPR, change management and shareholder value. He is a guest lecturer on the City University Business School's Evening MBA Programme and has lectured and spoken in many countries. He is also an advisor for The Prince's Trust. The numerous articles and books written by him include three other pocketbooks (on marketing, business planning and decision making), 'Financial Services – 1992' (Eurostudy) and 'Marketing for Success' and 'Value Pricing', both published by Kogan Page and, with 'The Marketing Pocketbook', written in conjunction with Dr Tony Fletcher.

Contact

You can reach the author on this E-mail: neiljones@neilsweb.fsnet.co.uk

关于作者
尼尔·罗素·仲斯

尼尔,是一位获得 MBA 学位的管理顾问。他是一位特许银行家并且是战略设计协会的一员。他与很多企业有跨国合作,特别是在战略、BPR、变革管理和股东价值领域。作为伦敦城大学商业学院 MBA 晚间课程的特邀演讲者,他在很多国家作了演讲和发言。他还是王子信托公司的顾问。在他的诸多著作中还包括其他三本袖珍笔记(关于市场、商业策划和策略制定)、《金融服务——1992》(欧洲研究)、《成功市场学》和《价值评估》,均由科根·佩奇公司出版,他还与托尼·弗莱彻博士合著过《市场学手册》。

联系方式
可以通过 E-mail 与作者联系:
E-mail: neiljones@ neilsweb. fsnet. co. uk

读者意见反馈卡

感谢您购买本书,请您填妥下表,以便我们今后为您提供更好的图书。

书名:《英汉对照管理袖珍手册:管理变革》

请填写(或附名片):

姓名:　　　　　　　　　　　邮编:

E-Mail:　　　　　　　　　　电话:

年龄:　　　　　　　　　　　职业:

地址:

1. 您认为本书采用英汉对照的方式对您的学习有帮助吗?

　　有　　　　　　　　　没有

2. 您希望本书采用何种方式?

　　全部中文　　　　　　　全部英文　　　　　　　英汉对照

3. 您认为本书翻译质量如何?

　　很好　　　　　　　　　尚可　　　　　　　　　较差

4. 您从何处购得此书？

书店　　邮购　　商场　　其他：＿＿＿＿＿＿＿＿＿＿

5. 您是如何得知本书的？（请在画线处写上报纸或杂志的名称）

书店　　朋友　　报纸：＿＿＿＿＿＿＿＿　　杂志：＿＿＿＿＿＿＿＿

其他：＿＿＿＿＿＿＿＿

6. 您喜欢本书的封面吗？

喜欢　　　　　　　　　　不喜欢

7. 您认为本书的价格：

偏高　　　　　　　　中等　　　　　　　　　　偏低

您的目标价位是：＿＿＿＿＿＿

8. 您认为本书的翻译有重大错误吗？如果有，请填写或用其他方式与我们联系：

＿＿＿＿＿＿＿＿＿＿＿＿＿＿＿＿＿＿＿＿＿＿＿＿＿＿＿＿＿＿＿＿

＿＿＿＿＿＿＿＿＿＿＿＿＿＿＿＿＿＿＿＿＿＿＿＿＿＿＿＿＿＿＿＿

如有任何疑问和要求，请与我们联系：

上海交通大学出版社　　　　　　　　　　电话：021-61675269

地址：上海市番禺路 951 号　　　　　　　邮编：200030

电子邮箱：wangliatcn@gmail.com（邮件主题请写丛书名或书名）

联系人：汪俪

英汉对照管理袖珍手册(第1辑)

英汉对照管理袖珍手册(第 2 辑)

英汉对照管理袖珍手册(第 3 辑)

46	创意经理人	☐	49	语音技巧	☐
47	卓越销售	☐	50	电子客户关怀	☐
48	提高利润率	☐			

本丛书可在当当、卓越、京东等网店购买。

1. 如需邮购,请将汇款寄至:

   上海市番禺路 951 号,上海交通大学出版社读者服务部 收

   邮编:200030 电话:021-61675298

   请在汇款留言中写明所购图书品种以及数量。国内邮寄免收邮费。

2. 也可在书名后的方框内填上购买册数,传真至读者服务部。

   传真:021-61675267

已推出盒套装(50 种),定价:500 元